CASH MONEY:
OPPORTUNITY MONEYMAKING BOOK

Book 2—Connections

Minister Dr. Joyce D. Shearin

Order this book online at www.trafford.com
or email orders@trafford.com

Most Trafford titles are also available at major online book retailers.

Print information available on the last page.

ISBN: 978-1-4907-9154-8 (sc)
ISBN: 978-1-4907-9160-9 (e)

Trafford rev. 10/12/2018

 www.trafford.com

North America & international
toll-free: 1 888 232 4444 (USA & Canada)
fax: 812 355 4082

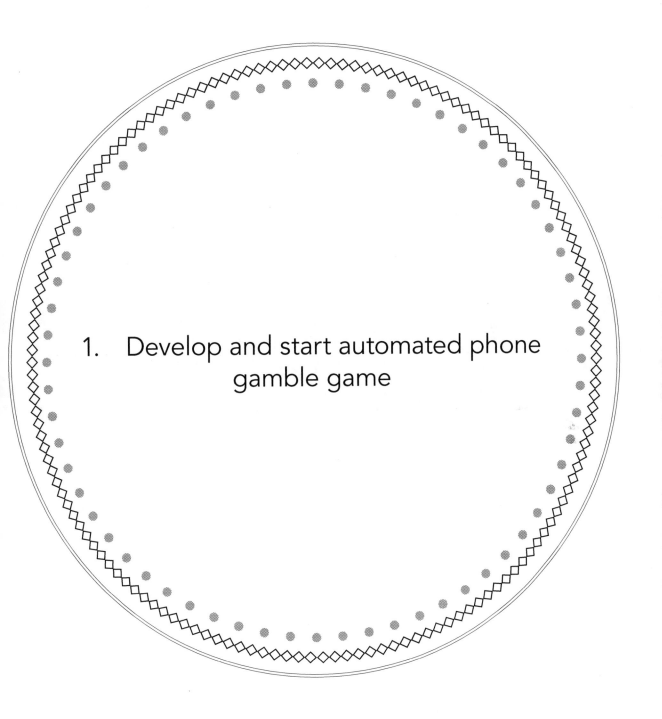

1. Develop and start automated phone gamble game

2. Casino Website – Get all required Licensing

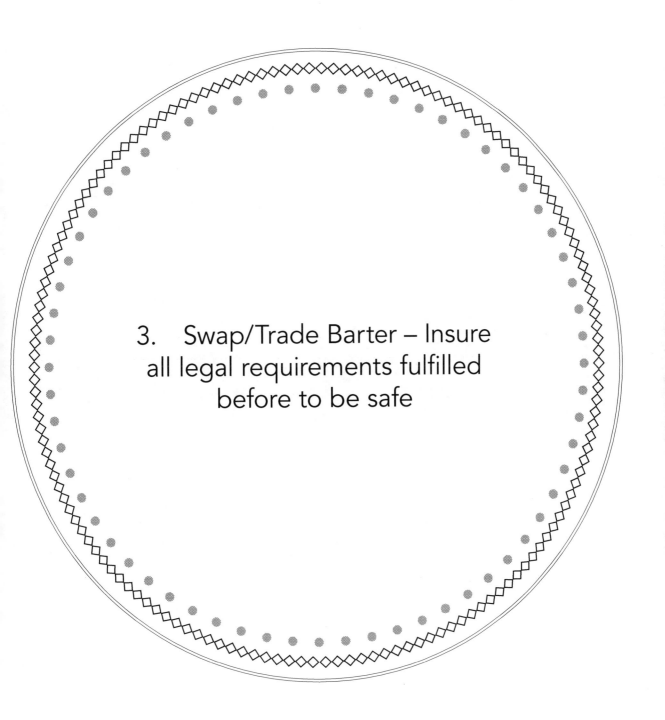

3. Swap/Trade Barter – Insure
all legal requirements fulfilled
before to be safe

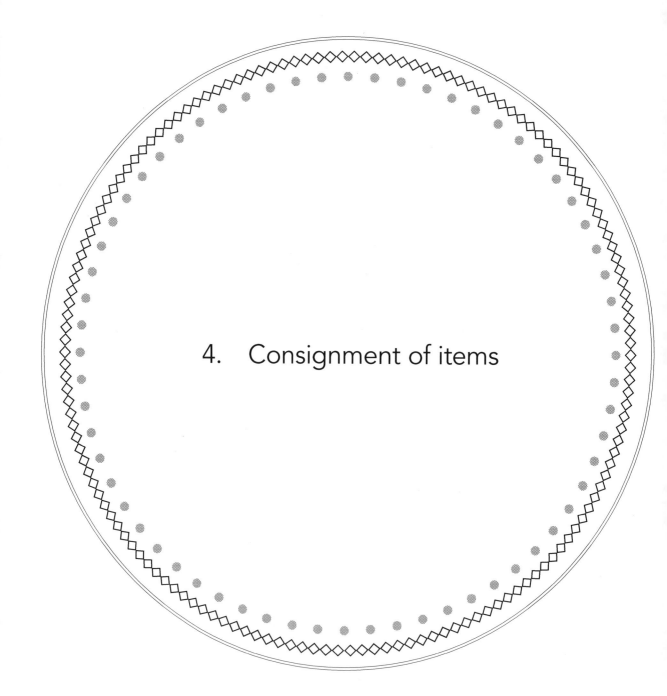

4.   Consignment of items

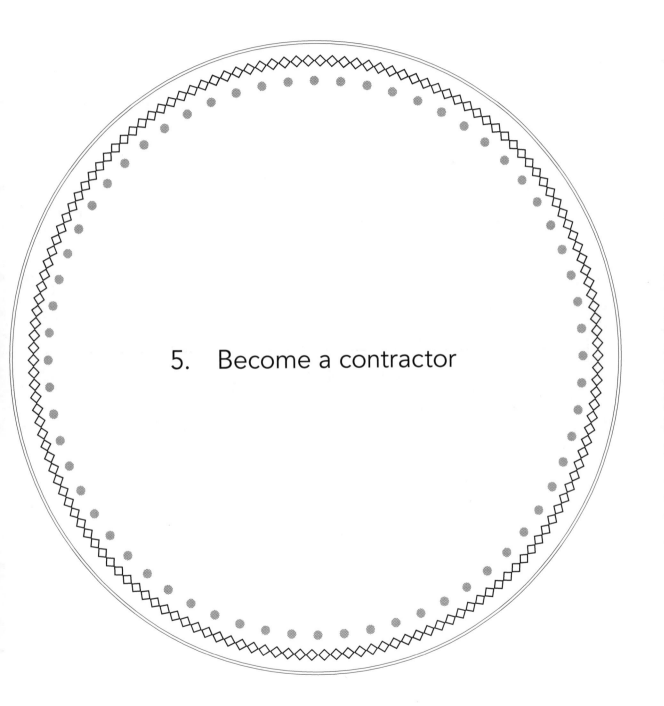

5.   Become a contractor

6.   Become an independent news consultant for info.

7. Start a mini-lawyer school with
certification on site and
new associations.

8. Do laundry delivery and pick up service.

9. Offer in proper places to help/assist
for a small fee (care aides)

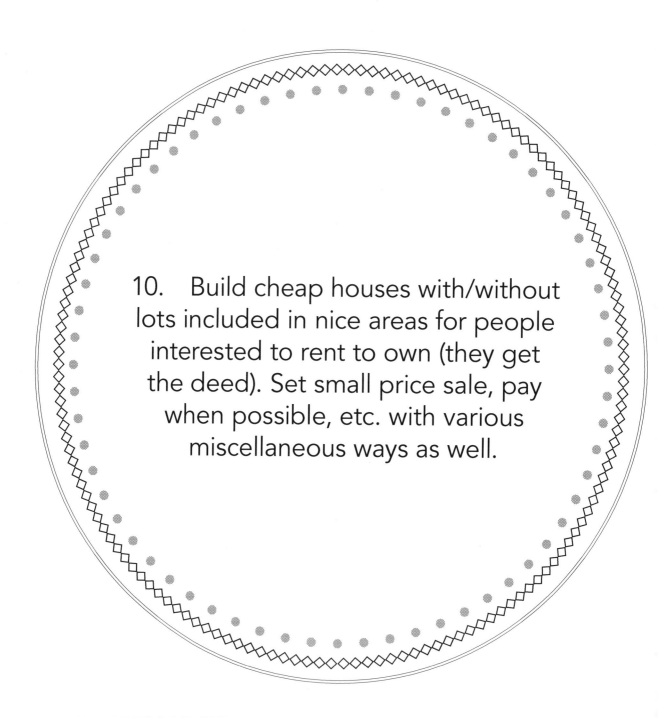

10.   Build cheap houses with/without lots included in nice areas for people interested to rent to own (they get the deed). Set small price sale, pay when possible, etc. with various miscellaneous ways as well.

11.   Start a good membership nonviolent with/without a cause and charge a small fee, get donations, etc.

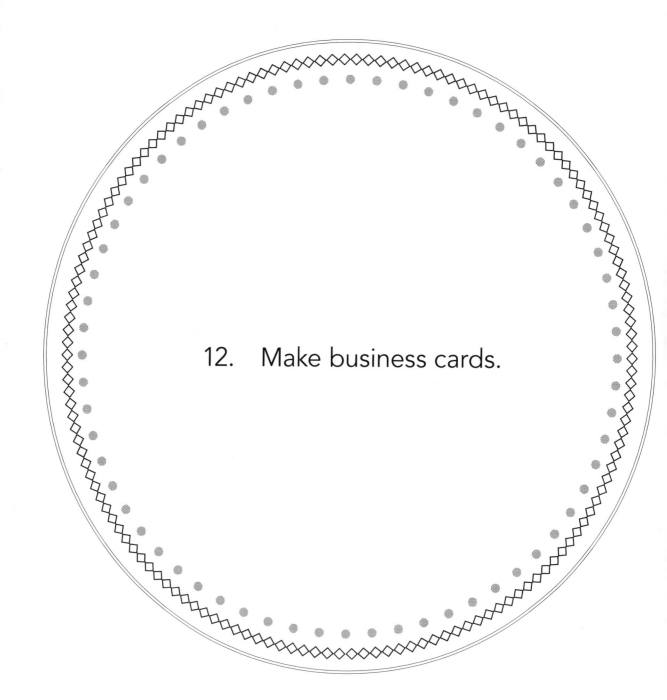

12.　Make business cards.

13. Start/do a cleaning service.

14.   Do raffles.

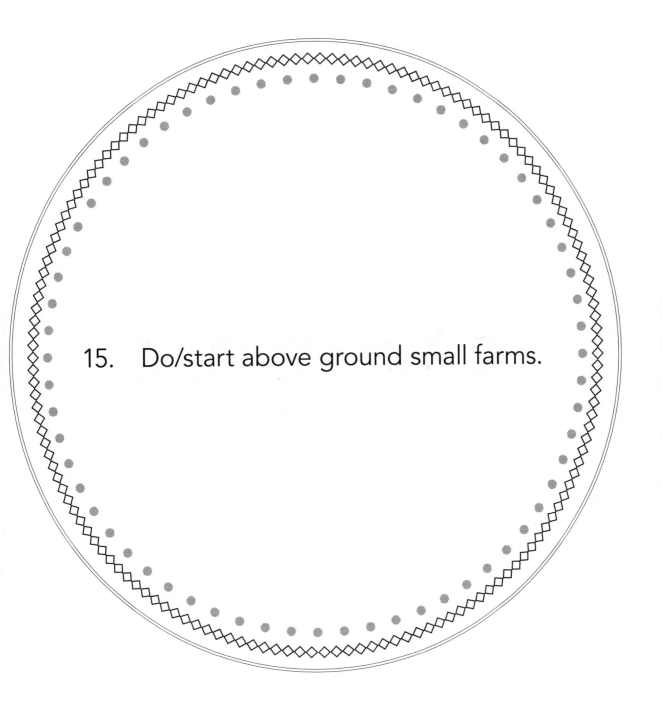

15. Do/start above ground small farms.

16.   Become a doctor/lawyer for
yourself. Practice a little if needed.

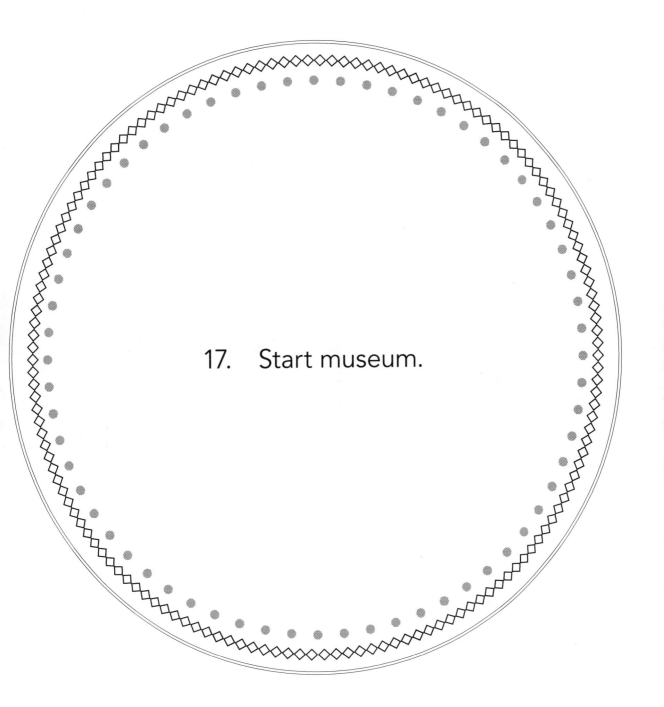

17.   Start museum.

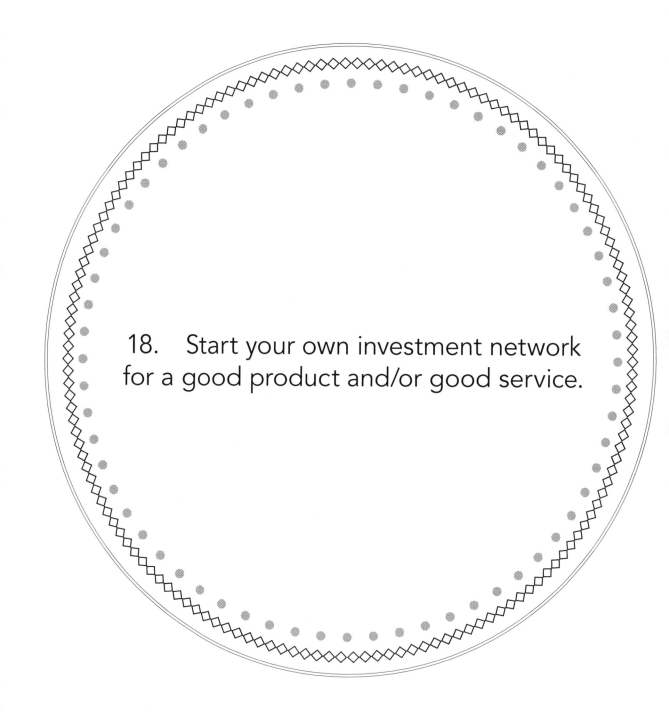

18.   Start your own investment network for a good product and/or good service.

19.   Become a minister.

20.   Become a vendor.

21.   Become a chef.

22. Become a homeowner.

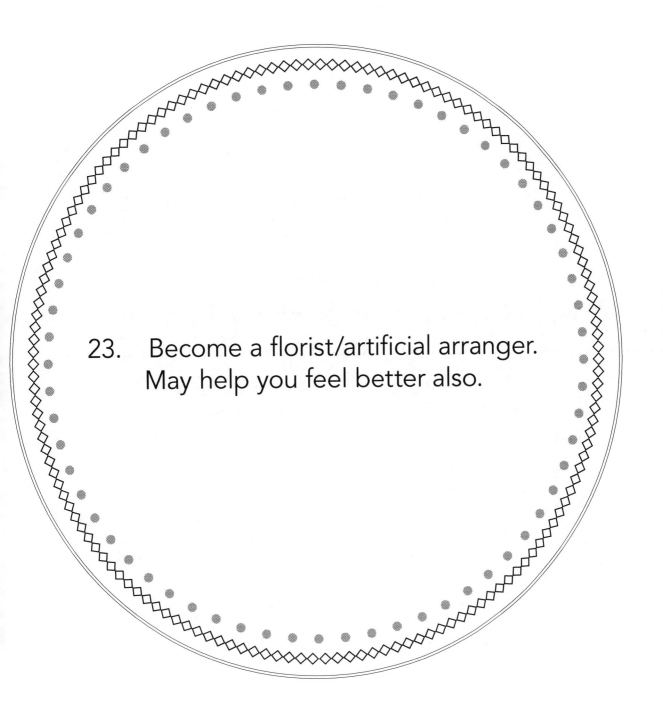

23.   Become a florist/artificial arranger.
May help you feel better also.

24.   Found a foundation for a fee with a good purpose like build homes for military veterans for a nominal price or fee.

25. Form your own local sports team with games for your team.

26.   Form a new concept or profession.

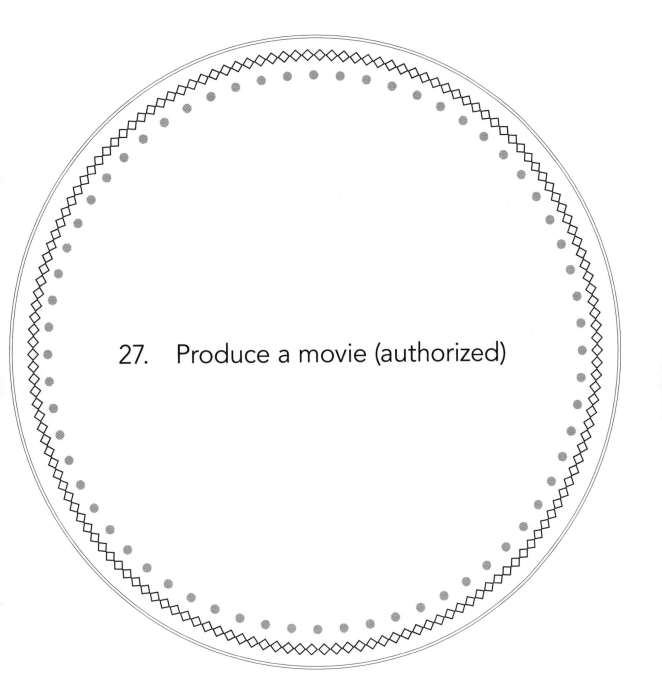

27.   Produce a movie (authorized)

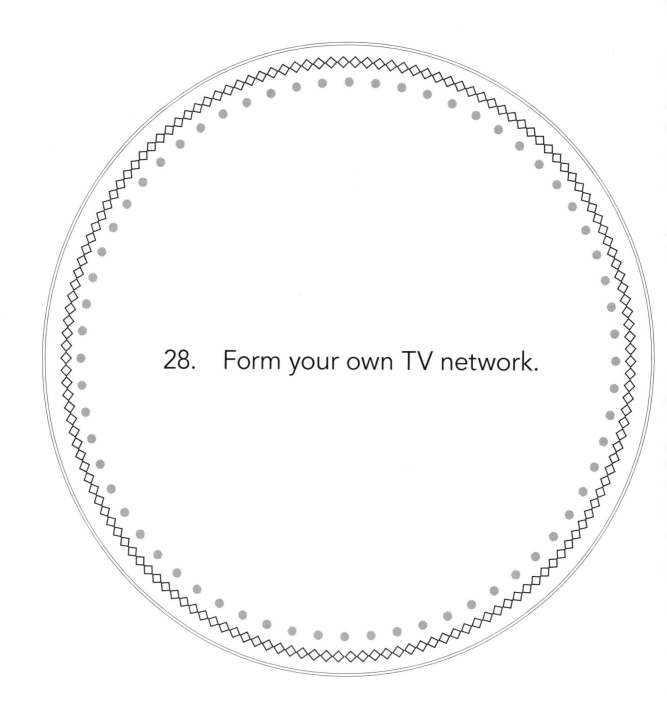

28. Form your own TV network.

29. Do a theatre production.

30. Develop your own awards categories for a fee/nominal amount.

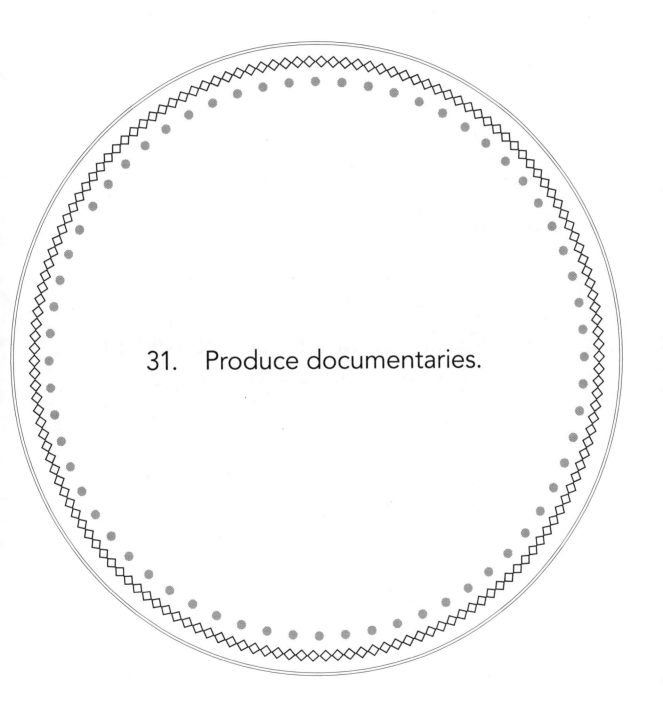

31.   Produce documentaries.

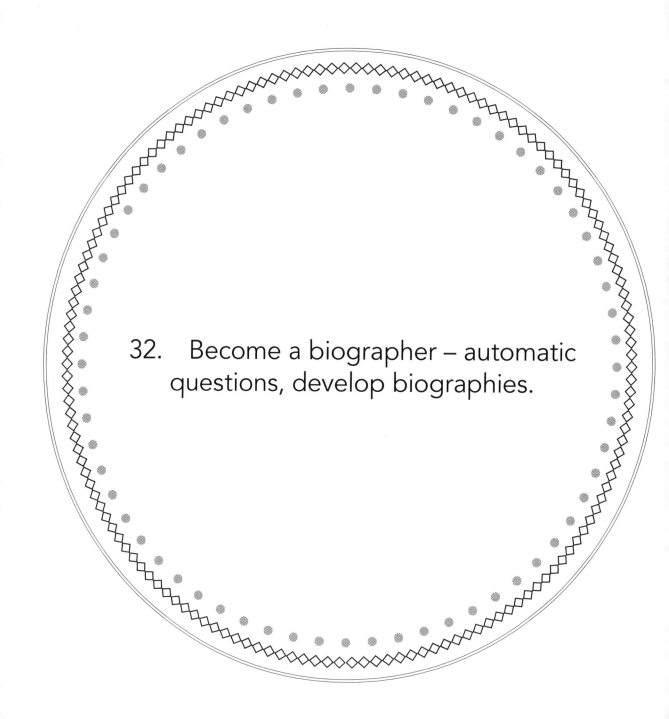

32. Become a biographer – automatic questions, develop biographies.

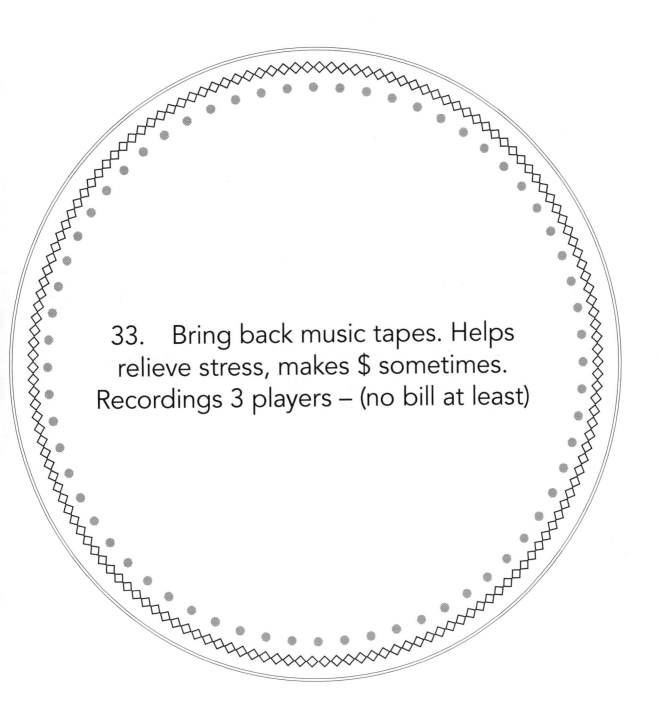

33. Bring back music tapes. Helps
relieve stress, makes $ sometimes.
Recordings 3 players – (no bill at least)

34. Form a new lawyers' group/
association.

35.   Become a phone technologist – for government and private US industry.

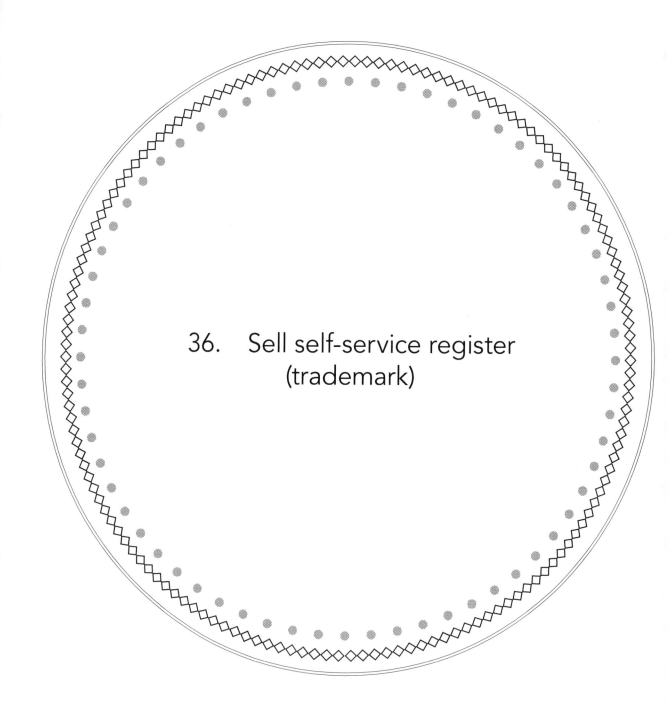

36.　Sell self-service register
(trademark)

37.   Sell pizza/make pizza wraps/tacos.

38.   Do a pizza bar/taco bar.

39.   Become a teacher in your own school through online or mail correspondence.

40.   Make/do a game self-operating
small machine.

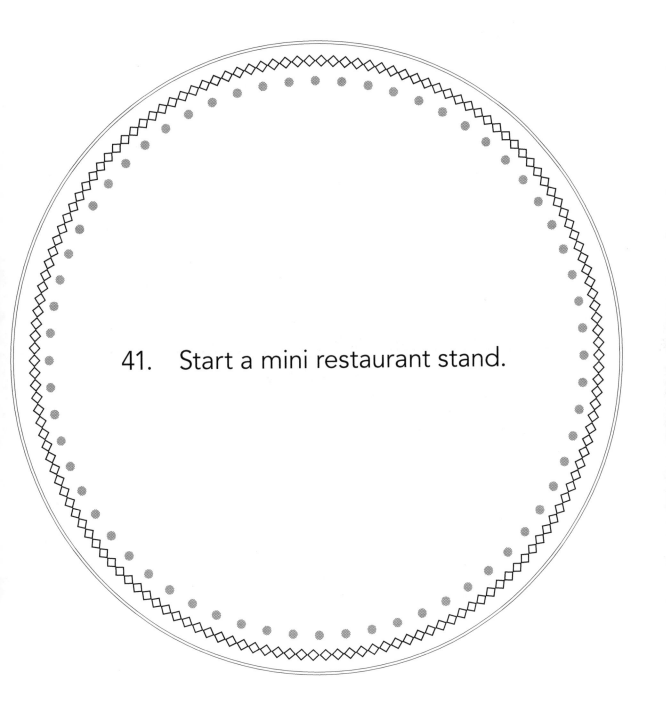

41.   Start a mini restaurant stand.

42. Help with home repairs for a small fee.

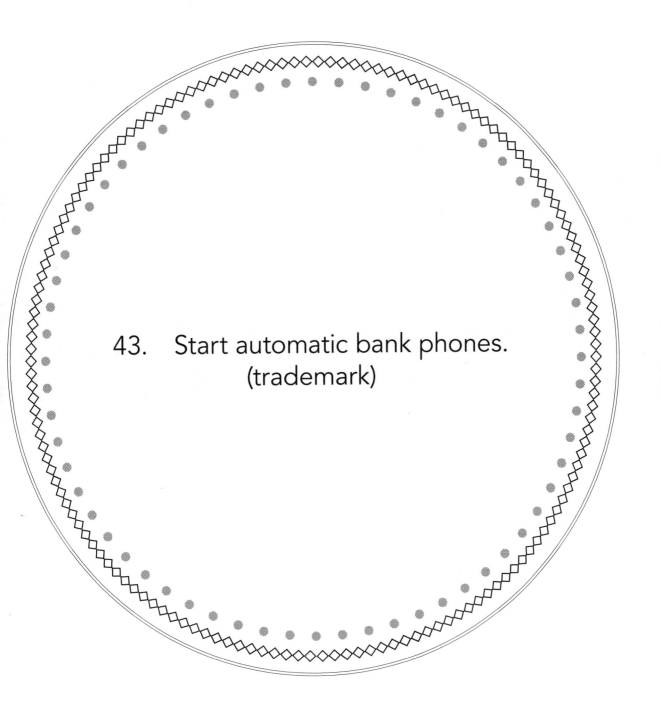

43. Start automatic bank phones.
(trademark)

44. Get/develop more microwaveable food to save $ on bills.

45. Become a financial consultant.

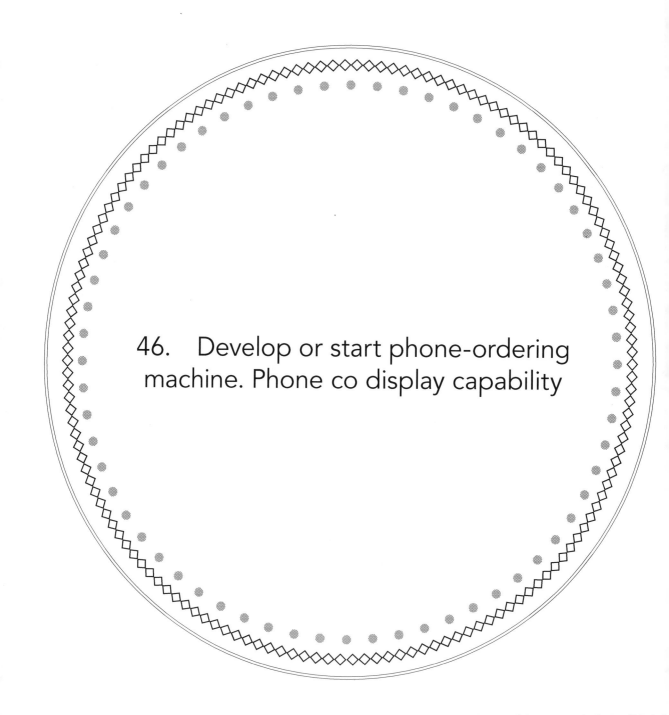

46. Develop or start phone-ordering machine. Phone co display capability

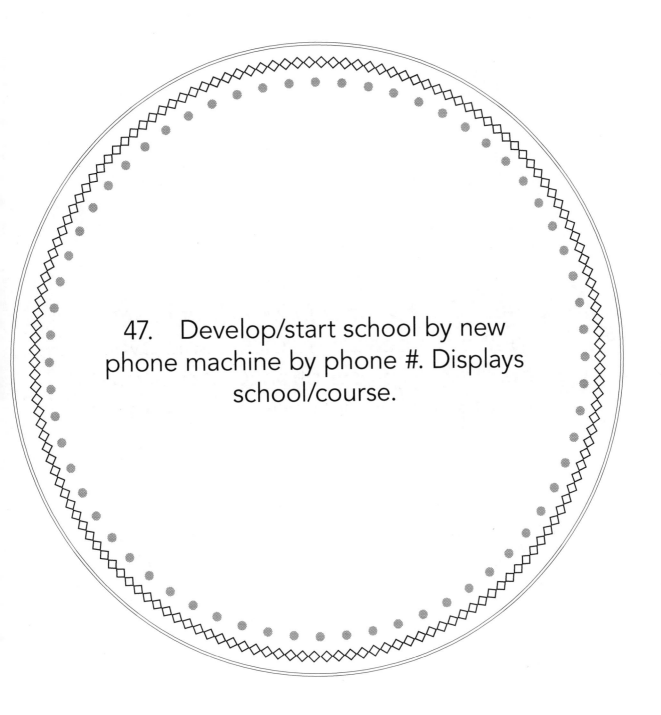

47. Develop/start school by new phone machine by phone #. Displays school/course.

48. Start your own legal legitimate brand of cheaper medicine sold over the counter/prescription (Optional due to health/medical side crisis need)

49. Start a visiting doctor/visiting lawyer group in the USA.

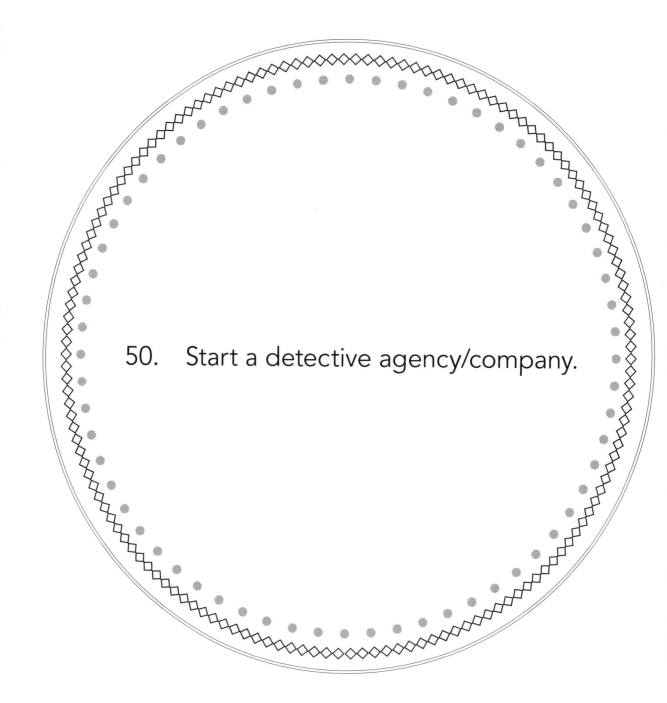

50.   Start a detective agency/company.

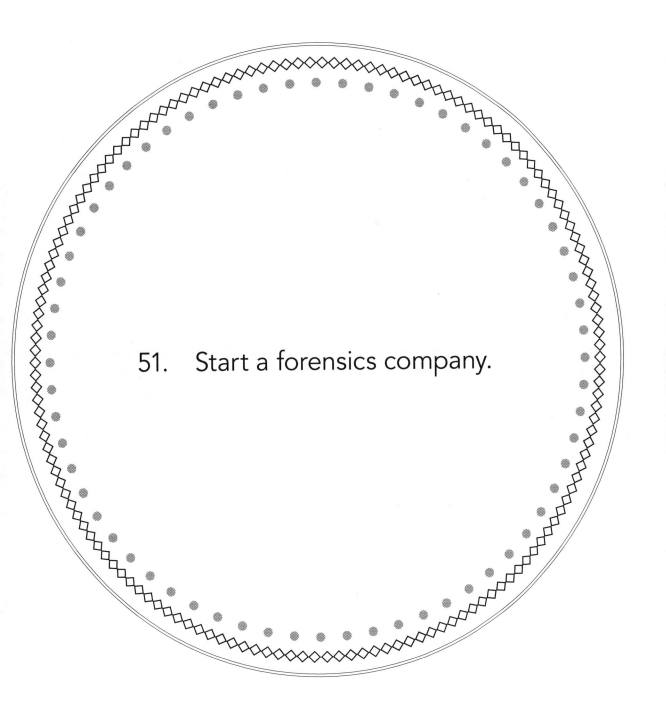

51.	Start a forensics company.

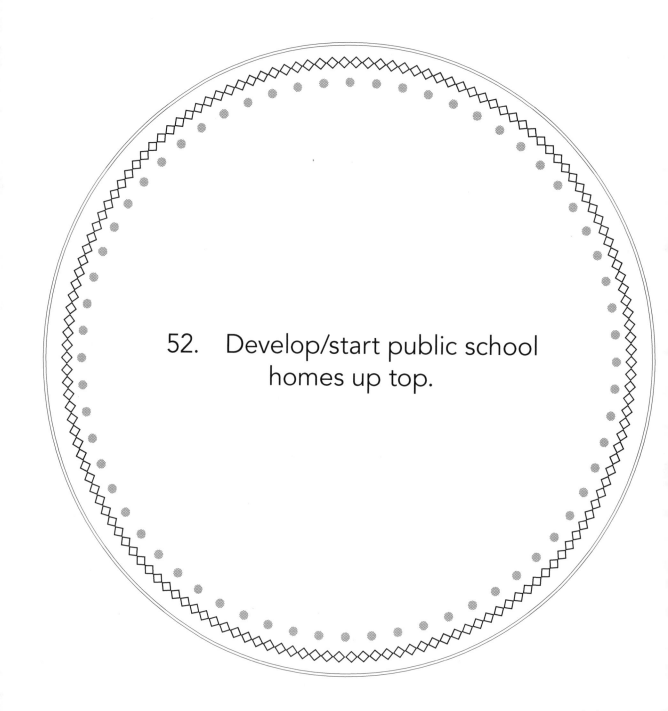

52. Develop/start public school homes up top.

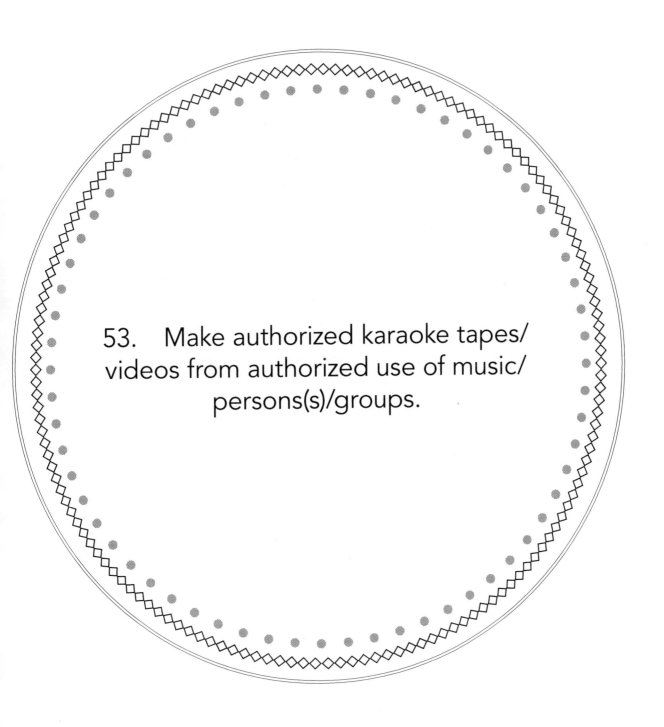

53.   Make authorized karaoke tapes/
videos from authorized use of music/
persons(s)/groups.

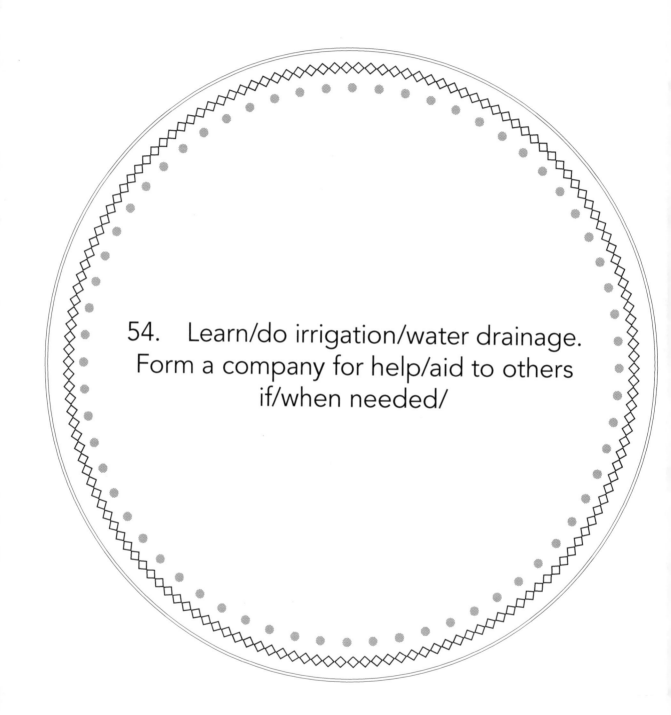

54. Learn/do irrigation/water drainage.
Form a company for help/aid to others
if/when needed/

55. Do/start library bookstores. Please feature and sell all my books.

56.   Start a pizza chain. Cheap
structured with loan, land, building
assistance if needed.

57. Do a cheese/lemonade stand.

58. Open/sell music in a record shop. Helps heal and helps relieve stress sometimes.

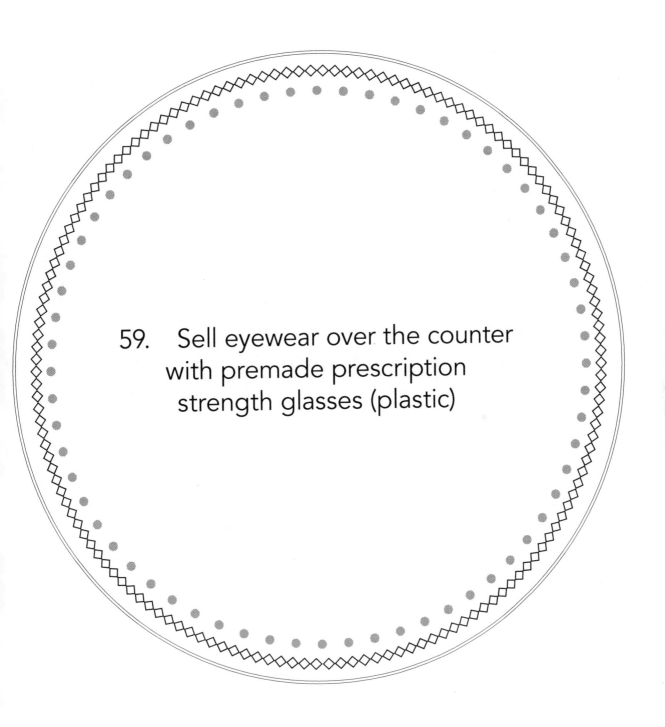

59. Sell eyewear over the counter
with premade prescription
strength glasses (plastic)

60. Start visiting instructors.

61. Start visiting schools.

62. Become a judge (personal enrichment, contest, law, etc.)

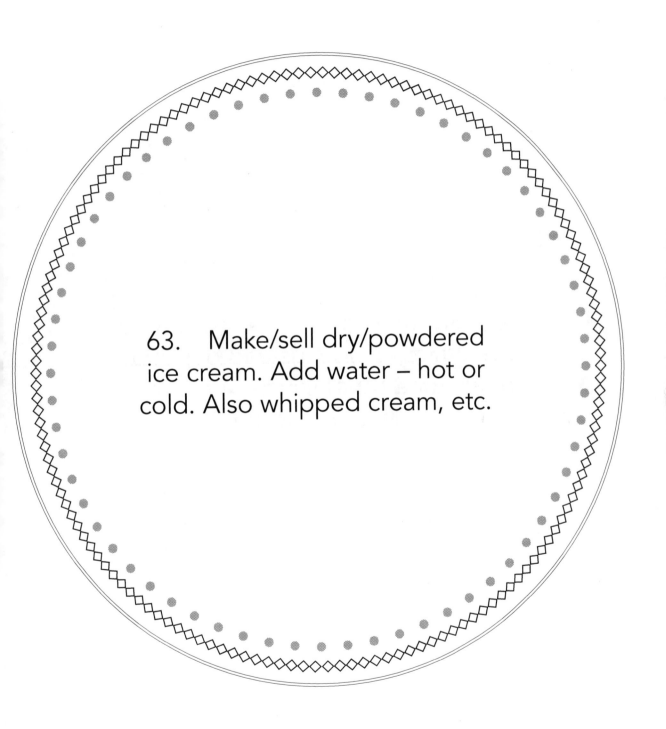

63.   Make/sell dry/powdered ice cream. Add water – hot or cold. Also whipped cream, etc.

64. Start/sell/make tuna barbeque. Healthier for you instead of pork/ beef. (tuna & hot sauce with mayo/ coleslaw if desired)

65. Become a dancer.

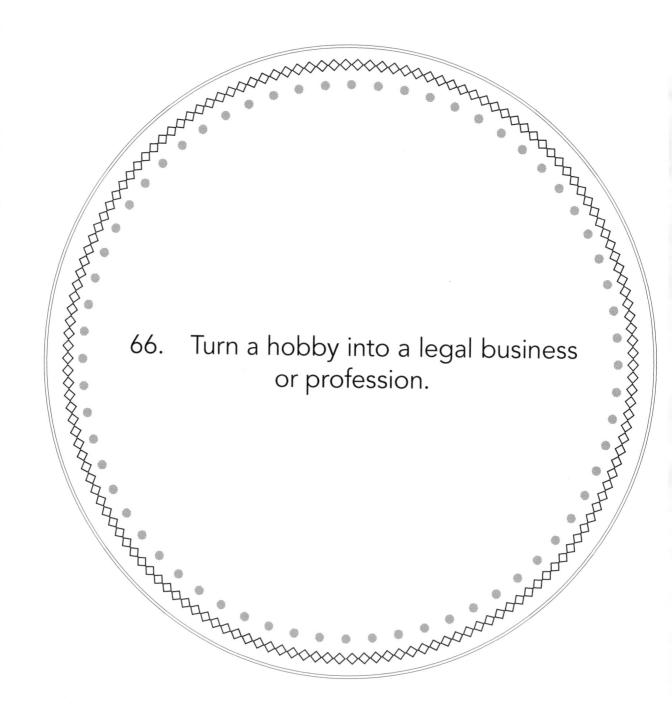

66. Turn a hobby into a legal business or profession.

Printed in the United States
By Bookmasters